*Those of us who do good are like an orchard
full of the fruit of good works.*

HILDEGARD OF BINGEN

SPIRITUAL LESSONS FROM AN

Apple Orchard

Fiona MacMath

OLIVER NELSON

THOMAS NELSON PUBLISHERS

Published in Nashville, Tennessee, by Thomas Nelson, Inc.,
Publishers, and distributed in Canada by Word Communications, Ltd.,
Richmond, British Columbia.

The Bible version used in this publication is
THE NEW KING JAMES VERSION.

Copyright © 1979, 1980, 1982, 1990, Thomas Nelson Inc., Publishers.

LIBRARY OF CONGRESS CATOLOGING-IN-PUBLICATION DATA
MacMath, Fiona.
Spiritual lessons from an apple orchard / Fiona MacMath.
p.   cm.
ISBN 0-7852-7609-2
1. Spiritual life--Christianity. 2. Apple--Relgious aspects--Christianity.
3. MacMath, Fiona. I. Title.
BV4501.2.M4359   1996

248.4--dc20   95-4787
                                                                  CIP

Printed and bound in Singapore.

1 2 3 4 5 6 — 01 00 99 98 97 96

CONTENTS

INTRODUCTION

Throughout ancient literature and the Bible, loving references are made to fruit of all kinds, but especially the apple, whose cultivation was an art. The apple of discord led to the fall of Troy. Hercules braved the dragon with a hundred heads to gather the golden apples of the Hesperides. The Scandinavian gods remained immortal by tasting the apple of eternal youth. And Prince Ahmed's apple in the *Arabian Nights* could cure every illness.

The medieval and Renaissance poets saw in the apple a symbol of life, death, beauty, love, indeed, of Christ Himself. In the seventeenth century, a gardener called Ralph Austin wrote a treatise called *The Spiritual Uses of an Orchard, or Garden of Fruits*, the title of which inspired this twentieth-century meditation on Christian life and growth.

> *The trees of nature fruitless be*
> *Compared with Christ the apple tree.*
>
> ELIZABETH POSTERN

PLANTING THE ORCHARD 1

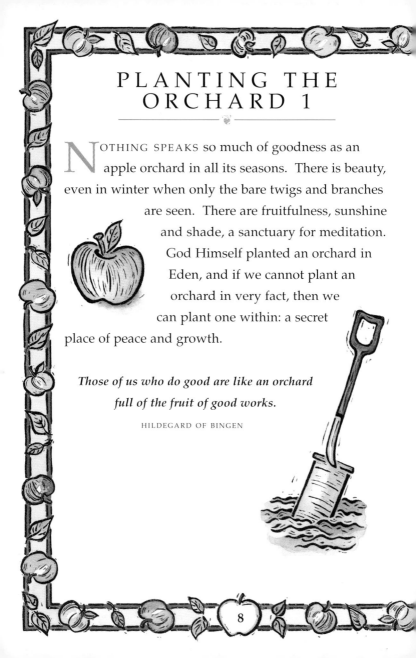

NOTHING SPEAKS so much of goodness as an apple orchard in all its seasons. There is beauty, even in winter when only the bare twigs and branches are seen. There are fruitfulness, sunshine and shade, a sanctuary for meditation. God Himself planted an orchard in Eden, and if we cannot plant an orchard in very fact, then we can plant one within: a secret place of peace and growth.

Those of us who do good are like an orchard full of the fruit of good works.

HILDEGARD OF BINGEN

PLANTING THE
ORCHARD 2

To PREPARE the orchard, the gardener should work
the ground with manure and compost. Heavy,
waterlogged soil may dispose some varieties to canker,
and sandy, stony soil will cause poor, undersized fruit.

Past experiences, good and bad, can be transformed
into rich ground for new growth. A dull, miserable
faith will produce only a dull, diseased soul; a shallow
life, full of distractions, will have little fruit to show at
the end.

VARIETIES

THERE ARE some 2,500 varieties of apple in the British National collection, and a similar number in the New York State collection, each with different habits, colors, flavors, scents, and sweetnesses. Some would be worth growing for their beautiful names alone: in England the Reinette, Orange Pippin, Golden Pippin, Russet, Norfolk Biffin, Blenheim Orange, Beauty of Bath, D'Arcy Spice; in North America the Maiden's Blush, Northern Spy, Winesap, and Wolf River. Who can say which one might have been the luscious, tempting apple in the Garden of Eden? It was certainly not the leathery-skinned Granny Smith or the Golden Delicious, groomed out of all natural flavor and texture.

When choosing varieties to plant, think of the space available, their keeping qualities, their pollination and, above all, their scent and flavor.

The apostle Paul exhorts his brothers and sisters in Corinth to value each other for their variety of gifts. Such variety comes from God, who delights to create in a myriad of forms. Variety is precious. Do not seek to impose uniformity on others, for they are individuals, endowed with different characteristics and gifts, and precious in God's sight.

Further, do not expect of yourself *all* the gifts that you admire in others. Each variety is valuable for itself, and we don't look for anything beyond natural perfection in each apple of its kind. Neither should we expect in ourselves the full perfection of opposites. If we do, disappointment is inevitable.

GRAFTING 1

Aʟʟ ᴏᴜʀ varieties of eating apple are thought to have developed originally from the wild crab apple, the *Malus saeversii*, a native of the Caucusus, and good trees are still made from grafting a cultivated variety onto a strong root stock from the wild apple.

The Christian faith did not spring, ready formed, from Christ's lips. Rather, it grew from Judaism, Christ's own faith.

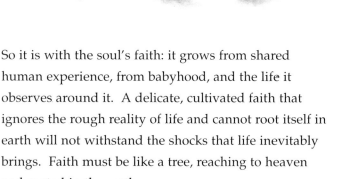

So it is with the soul's faith: it grows from shared human experience, from babyhood, and the life it observes around it. A delicate, cultivated faith that ignores the rough reality of life and cannot root itself in earth will not withstand the shocks that life inevitably brings. Faith must be like a tree, reaching to heaven and rooted in the earth.

GRAFTING 2

CHRISTIANS ARE apt to see themselves as more perfect than people who worship God in a different way. They may think that they, being the later branch of religion, have been grafted onto earlier beliefs.

The apostle Paul uses the image of a wild branch being grafted onto an olive tree to explain how Christian faith has grown out of the Jewish faith.

He deplored the branch's sense of superiority toward the stock. He warns the Romans that what has been grafted in may be taken out, and the life of the grafted branch depends upon life flowing up through the root stock. God's life flows through both stock and branch to bear fruit. All branches must have mutual respect because they have the same life source.

PLANTING THE ORCHARD 3

E ACH VARIETY of apple will grow to its own perfect size and shape, given enough space. Crowded trees will not attain their full potential. Yet growing several compatible trees together will enhance pollination and afford shelter from strong winds.

For healthy growth, the right balance of space and companionship is essential. As with apple trees, so with people.

WALLS

THE BEST orchards will be walled. This is a costly undertaking, and yet it is worth it in the end to protect the apple trees from winds and thieves, and to create a haven of peace. The walled garden is an ancient symbol of the soul—precious, secret, known only to God.

A garden enclosed is my sister, my spouse,
A spring shut up, a fountain sealed.
Your plants are an orchard of pomegranates
With pleasant fruits, fragrant henna with spikenard,
Spikenard and saffron, calamus and cinnamon,
With all trees of frankincense, myrrh and aloes,
With all the chief spices—a fountain of gardens,
A well of living waters, and streams from Lebanon.

Awake, O north wind, and come, O south!
Blow upon my garden, that its spices may flow out.
Let my beloved come to his garden and eat its
pleasant fruits.

SONG OF SOLOMON 4:12–16

YOUNG TREES

ESTABLISHED APPLE trees can be left, for the most part, without harm. But newly planted trees must be firmly trodden in and staked to withstand winds and frost. They need faithful watering and pruning; they are not to be expected to bear much fruit. Grass around their roots will starve them, and it is better to keep a two- to three-foot radius of clear soil around the trees until their roots are well established. Otherwise they may need extra nitrogen.

So with young souls. They need freedom to grow, security, and support; inspiration from other, older souls, nourishment, and loving attention. It is not to be expected that they should give greatly at first, but only to show promise of growth and fruitfulness in years to come.

FROST IN MAY

A TREE laden with precocious blossoms and promising a rich harvest to come may have all its autumn fruit nipped in the bud by a late frost. Too great blossoming too early may be quickly withered and destroyed. It is better that spring comes slowly but surely, leading on to a full, rich maturity.

TRAINED
APPLE TREES

IT IS possible to train apple trees along walls or wire fences or as single- or double-stemmed cordons. This allows the gardener to tend smaller numbers of fruit more carefully, gather them easily, and grow more varieties in a smaller space. Some enjoy a row of neat cordon-trained trees, or an old brick wall with espaliers spread along it. But the standard trees are both beautiful and undemanding and give a more plentiful crop.

Trained trees are like spiritual athletes. Some are called to such a life and should never be despised for willingly enduring privations and limitations in order to bear their few but precious fruit. For most souls, making the most of what life has to offer them, with all its possibilities and freedom, is not to be forsworn but to be abundantly enjoyed.

TRUE BEAUTY

NOTHING CAN match apple blossom in spring, pink-and-white flowers lavishly piled on every branch, as mouthwatering as strawberries and cream to come, drifting to the ground as white flakes to make of the grass a starry midnight sky. It is more generous than pear blossom, and more delicate than may blossom, but without the languid overblown beauty of the flowering cherry.

And unlike the flowering cherry, the apple blossom is full of promise of fruit to come; not showy, useless little fruit, good only for birds to peck at, but grand, sweet-scented apples to feed birds and beasts and the grateful gardener. Why do people choose to plant those barren suburban beauties when they could have both beauty and goodness from the humble homegrown apple?

BIRDS
AND BLOSSOMS

BIRDS ARE beautiful creatures, but some of them are a nuisance when the apple trees are in bloom, for they like to destroy the flowers. Nevertheless, they are easily frightened away by strips of silver paper attached to the branches.

When the soul begins to blossom under the Gardener's care, there are always a few people who take pleasure in trying to destroy its new good growth. Even other Christian souls are often jealous of the signs of the Spirit's welling up life in another, especially if their own progress seems slow and unremarkable. They are not so easily frightened away.

SEASONS OF
THE SPIRIT 1

SOME PEOPLE experience the
spiritual life as a gradual
progression through the seasons. There
is the first quickening, the beauty of
which will never quite be matched again.
Old habits and fears are joyfully cast aside as the
sudden dawning of light grows more intense. Lives
blossom in a thousand different ways,
and friends can only marvel at the
transformation.

But all too soon, rough winds strip
the blossoms from the tree. For a while, nothing but
the slow green leaves are seen, and one could think
that, for all its past finery, there is no real progress
being made. Only time and patience will show
whether or not the fruit has set, and whether, come
autumn, splendid fruit will appear.

SEASONS OF
THE SPIRIT 2

FOR SOME, the seasons take a lifetime to develop. Youth is a time of splendid achievement; middle age is a hard struggle through the daily and nightly tasks of doing business and bringing up a family. The true value and worth of that life are apparent only later on.

For others, there is a constant cycle from the glorious optimism of springtime, life and fruiting time, to the deadness of winter, which often without warning bursts into a greater blossoming than ever before.

To everything there is a season,
A time for every purpose under heaven:
A time to be born,
And a time to die;
A time to plant,
And a time to pluck what is planted.

ECCLESIASTES 3:1–2

ROOTS

WE SEE and wonder at the apple tree for its beauty and fruitfulness, but no one sees the source of life deep below the ground. That is where the goodness and moisture are continually taken in through the branching networks of roots, as great as, if not greater than, the tree itself. Without this active but unseen life, there would be no life at all in the tree. Why, then, is it surprising that in every alive, attractive, growing person, there is a source of life hidden from sight?

BARK RINGING

I F THERE is much growth but little blossom and small promise of fruit to come, the gardener must check the tree's growth.   In Maytime, a thin strip of bark, about half an inch wide, is cut from around the too-vigorous branch, or from the main trunk if the whole tree is making too much growth. The ring is then sealed with tape to protect it from infection.

The soul is apt to forget its true purpose and take its own direction, especially when everything seems to smile upon it. The Gardener may well give a slight check, a small wound, to redirect the soul's efforts toward its true purpose.

SUNLIGHT

THE APPLE trees need good soil and rain. But without sunlight, too, the apples will not ripen finely.

Although the soul needs prayer and discipline to grow straight and well, it needs its measure of sunlight —happiness—too, if it is to have energy for growth and sweetness in its maturity. A joyless Christian must be a contradiction in terms. Jesus promised those who would come to Him that His yoke would be easy, His burden light. If we find our souls becoming heavy or dull, we must ask for different graces: laughter, lightness, a sense of humility (which is good ground for a sense of humor), and a sense of God's companionship.

WAITING

SOULS ARE apt to become impatient with themselves, wishing by their own efforts to force the fruit and wring apples from the branches even as the blossom falls. The Gardener knows better, being content to see His trees grow silently and unnoticed, but still following His purpose and plan.

PERFECT BEING

THE GARDENER loves the apple trees, each one for itself. They need to prove nothing, do nothing, be nothing except their own particular selves, living, growing, bearing fruit. All of their functions are right and good: growing, breathing, taking in food, reproducing.

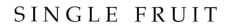

SINGLE FRUIT

To produce fruit for exhibition, the ambitious gardener will take all the fruit from each cluster, leaving only one single, perfect specimen.

Such single-mindedness is needed to achieve perfection. The soul ambitious for God will break off all other claims upon it that may sap its energy, all other distractions, no matter how good in themselves.

ABUNDANCE

MANY APPLE trees have two-year cycles, cropping poorly one year but abundantly the next: a time of scarcity heralds a time of plenty. The sight of trees weighted down with their own munificence reminds us of God's lavish generosity. Jesus promised not simply life, but life in abundance. The dry soul that longs to be like God must imitate that glorious, prodigal giving.

JESUS CHRIST
THE APPLE TREE

HOW FITTING to see Christ Himself as an apple tree! Nothing could, like Himself, be more familiar and yet so mysterious. His life, death, and resurrection offer to us all a remedy for the pains we suffer from the eating of the first apple—or all that that apple symbolizes. He is our food and drink, our shelter, our inspiration.

> *The trees of nature fruitless be*
> *Compared with Christ the apple tree.*
>
> ELIZABETH POSTERN

PICKING
THE APPLES

A S EACH fruit ripens, so it must be picked with great care, cradling it in one hand, holding the stalk with the other. If it comes away without reluctance, it is ready. But apples should never be pulled from the tree or wrenched off before they are fully ripened.

We desire a long, full life: to be "gathered to our fathers," as the Old Testament puts it, only when we have fulfilled our potential and grown to the full stature as people that God has planned for us.

WINDFALLS

SOME APPLES will always be blown down before they are fully ripened. These are food for wasps and birds, and nurseries for all manner of insects. But some will be the first apple pies and jellies. Some will rot gently into the ground to feed the parent tree, and the precious pips may sprout and grow in their turn. In God's economy, nothing is wasted.

TASTING THE FRUIT

IN LATE August or early September, the fruit have reached a young ripeness. What a pleasure it is to choose the first perfect apple, blushing rosily among the leaves, and to pluck it and smell its sharp, sweet scent! To polish it on a jacket sleeve, and then to taste the flesh—crisp, aromatic, and with its particular flavor. It is rare to find such a complete and perfect pleasure, one that has lasted since poor Adam and Eve stole the first. Now that we have other troubles enough, apples bring us only health and healing.

WASPS

ALTHOUGH THERE are painful times when accepting the fact is hard, wasps also have their place in the scheme of things. They are nature's scavengers and destroy many pests. The Gardener rejoices in all His creatures: none is to be hurt or wantonly destroyed.

But often the roundest, rosiest, most tempting blush conceals a rotten, hollow core, alive with angry wasps. Beware! Even the smallest creatures, going about God's business, have it in them to hurt others in their way.

THE WORM
IN THE APPLE

IT IS a perfect image of this world's fallenness: the seeming perfection of the apple and the horror of finding that perfect, glowing sphere full of black decay or wriggling with maggots. Josephus and Thevenot wrote of the apples of Sodom that grew on the shores of the Dead Sea. They appeared to be most delectable but turned to ashes in the mouth.

My soul was only apt and disposed to
great things; but souls to souls are like apples
to apples, one being rotten rots another.

THOMAS TRAHERNE

STORING APPLES

BY THE middle of October, all the apples should be gathered and stored carefully in a cool, dry, airy place. Old orchards often have picturesque apple houses: child-sized houses with slatted shelves for the apples to rest on. As a rule, the last apples to mature will also keep the longest, and these are worth wrapping in paper and keeping for the winter. The earliest maturing apples should be kept where they can be used first, and all should be checked regularly for disease and decay. Even the soundest-looking fruit may become rotten, and this will quickly spread to its healthy neighbors.

Goodness is catching. So is wickedness. Although the soul must radiate God's goodness to all about it, yet it must guard against the first, scarcely perceptible ways of evil.

GREASE-BANDS

MID-SEPTEMBER IS the time for amateur gardeners to place grease-bands on the apple trees to ward off winter pests. These are bands of greaseproof paper, about six inches wide, tied around the main trunk with string at about two feet from the ground. The paper is spread generously with grease (or a proprietary brand of paper and sticky compound can be bought), and this will trap the insects that crawl up the trunk to lay eggs on the branches and twigs. The grease-bands need to be inspected from time to time and regreased if necessary.

If only it were so easy to prevent troubles from invading the soul! Only through constant effort in prayer can these be discovered and struggled against before they wriggle into the bud. If something disturbs your peace or ruffles your faith, instead of stimulating and provoking it, guard against it.

PRUNING 1

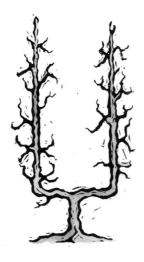

ACCURATE PRUNING is essential for espalier- and cordon-trained trees where a heavy crop is the first consideration. But for standard trees, only necessary thinning need be done to allow light and air to the center of the tree and to remove any dead or diseased wood.

Such cutting away of whatever would hold back the soul is vital for progress and fruitfulness. It is often said that the faith has grown greatest in times of persecution and that even in the life of the soul, greatest progress is made despite, or because of, sharp sorrow. If God allows pain and loss, it is always to give better direction and increase.

PRUNING 2

NOVEMBER IS the month for pruning standard apple trees. The gardener removes any branches that are overcrowding the center of the tree or growing across others. Any diseased branches are cut away also, and large wounds are painted with a dressing to prevent infection. Cutting away at all the small shoots is not necessary, and may encourage the tree to produce more in the following year. Rather, it is better to be bold and take out whole branches where necessary, and leave the rest alone.

Guilt likes to masquerade as humility and sanctity, but it produces only a sterile, useless self-regard. There is no need for the soul to endure endless, self-inflicted wounds; only to bear patiently those that are necessary for its best development, and those, we trust, to be quickly dealt with and healed by the Gardener.

PRUNING 3

ALL THE pruned wood should be taken away and burned. Otherwise it can become diseased, if it is not already, and will infect the tree.

"If your right hand causes you to sin," said Jesus, "cut it off." Such severity, such seriousness, is shocking. And yet it is the only sure way to protect ourselves from the temptations that continually drag on us like deadweights.

INSECTICIDES

N A still day at the end of December or the
beginning of January, when there is neither frost
nor wind, the apple trees may be sprayed with an
insecticide to kill off the eggs of caterpillars, aphids,
and apple suckers or *psyllides*.

Killing off of unwanted growth in the form of New
Year's resolutions might also take place on such a still
day at the turning of the year. And yet it will take
more than one application of heartfelt resolve to
destroy all of the old self-destructive habits that
develop imperceptibly but inevitably.

LIFE SPAN

ALL THINGS have their appointed life span: a time to grow and a time to die. Each leaf has less than a year to live, and most fruit the same, unless they be the wrinkled apple-Johns that keep for two years and reach their best in their old age. The apple trees grow for many years before they slowly weaken and die. But all pass through youth and maturity and decay, and show the beauty and purpose of each.

WINTER TREES

THE ORCHARD in winter is stripped and bare.
Only a few decaying windfalls may be left in the
frosty grass. Few people may visit it now, and even
the Gardener may seem to have abandoned it. But
while the trees seem dead and forgotten, that is only
an illusion. The branches are sleeping.

And deep in the earth, the roots faithfully keep life
alive until the coming of another springtime.

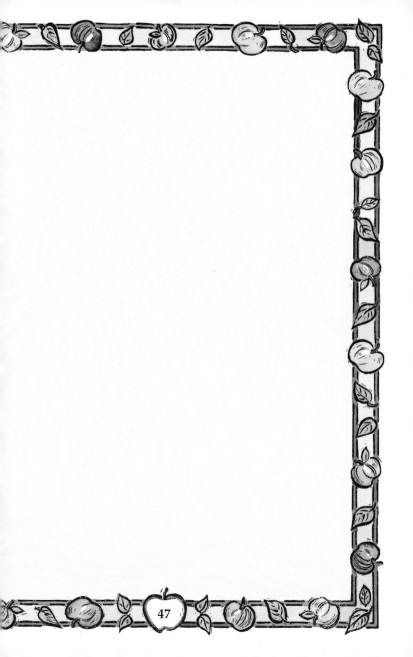